Contents

1. Program to print text

```c
# include <stdio.h>
# include <conio.h>
main()
{
clrscr();
printf("HELLO");
printf("Aditya Shakkarwar
phone : +91 8437164247");
getch();
}
```

2. Program To Read Two Numbers And Print The Sum Of Given Two Numbers.

```c
# include <stdio.h>
# include <conio.h>
main()
{
int a,b, sum;
clrscr ();
printf ("ENTER VALUE FOR A ;
");
scanf ("%d",&a);
printf("ENTER VALUE FOR B
;");
scanf("%d",&b);
sum=a+b;
printf("Sum Of Given Two
Numbers are %d", sum);
getch();
}
```

3. Program To Accept Student Roll No, Marks in 3 Subjects and Calculate Total, Average and Print it.

```c
# include <stdio.h>
# include <conio.h>
main()
{
int r,b,c,d, tot, avg;
clrscr();
printf ("ENTER STUDENT
ROLL NO ; ");
scanf ("%d",&r);
printf("ENTER FIRST
SUBJECT MARKS ;");
scanf("%d",&b);
printf("ENTER SECOND
SUBJECT MARKS;");
scanf("%d",&c);
printf("ENTER THIRD
```

```c
                                  SUBJECT MARKS ;");
scanf("%d",&d);
tot=b+c+d;
avg=tot/3;
printf("\n\n\t\t Lovely Professional University \n\n");
printf("\t STUDENT RNO ; %d
",r);
printf("\t FIRST SUBJECT
MARKS ;%d ",b);
printf("\t SECOND SUBJECT
MARKS ;%d ",C);
printf("\t THIRD SUBJECT
MARKS ;%d ",d);
printf("\t AVERAGE MARKS ;
%d", avg);
getch();
}
```

4. Program To Read Three Numbers And Print The Biggest Of Given Three Numbers

```c
#include <stdio.h>
# include <conio.h>
main( )
{
int a,b,c,big=0;
clrscr( );
printf("ENTER VALUE FOR A:");
scanf("%d",&a);
printf("ENTER VALUE FOR B:");
scanf("%d",&b);
print("ENTER VALUE FOR C:");
scanf("%d",&c);
if (a>big)
big=a ;
if(b>big)
big=b;
```

```c
if (c>big)

big=c;

printf ("BIGGEST OF ABOVE GIVEN THREE NUMBER IS %d",big)

getch( );
}
```

5. Program To Read A Number And Find Whether The Given Number Is Even Or Odd.

```c
# include <stdio.h>
# include <conio.h>
main()
{
int n,r;
clrscr();
printf("ENTER A NUMBER ;");
scanf("%d", &n);
r=n%2;
if(r= = 0)
printf("the above given number is even
number");
else
printf("the above given number is odd
number");
getch();
}
```

6. Program to accept a year and check whether the given year IS leap year or not.

```c
# include <stdio.h>
# include <conio.h>
main( )
{
int y;
clrscr( );
printf("enter a year:");
scanf("%d",&y);
if(y%4==0& &y%100!=0|| y%400==0);
printf("the above given year IS a leap
year");
else
printf("the above given year IS not a leap
year");
getch();
}
```

7. Individual Digits

```c
# include <stdio.h>
# include <conio.h>
main( )
{
int a,b,c,d;
clrscr( );
printf ( " Enter a two digit number :");
scanf (" %d", &a);
b=a/10;
c=a%10;
d=b+c;
printf ("sum of individual digits of givennumbers id %", d);
getch( );
}
```

8.   Program to accept a three digit number and print the sum of individual digits.

```c
# include <stdio.h>
# include <conio.h>
main( )
{
int a,b,c,n, sum;
clrscr( );
printf (" Enter a Three Digit Number:");
scanf ("%d",&n);
a=n/100;
b=( (n%100)/10);
c=n%10;
sum=a+b+c;
printf (" Sum of Individual Digits of
Given Numbers is %d", Sum);
getch( );
}
```

9. Program to accept a number and check the given number is Armstrong or not.

```c
# include <stdio.h>
# include <conio.h>
main( )
{
int n, a, b, c, d;
clrscr( );
printf (" Enter a Three Digit Number: ");
scanf ("%d", &n);
a=n/100;
b=((n/10)%10);
c=n%10;
d=a*a*a*+b*b*b +c*c*c;
if (n= =d)
printf ("The Given Number is Armstrong
number");
else
```

```c
printf ("The Given Number is Not
Armstrong number");
getch( );
}
```

10. Program to print ODD numbers from 1 to 10

```c
# include <stdio.h>
# include <conio.h>
main( )
{
int i;
clrscr( );
for (i=1; i<=10; i+=2)
printf("%d\n",i);
getch( );
}
```

11. Program to print natural numbers from 1 to 10 in Reverse

```c
# include <stdio.h>
# include <conio.h>
main( )
{
int i;
clrscr( );
for (i=10; i>=1; i--)
printf("%d\n",i);
getch( );
}
```

12. Program to print sum of the natural numbers from 1 to 10.

```c
# include <stdio.h>
# include <conio.h>
main( )
{
int n,sum=0,i;
clrscr( );
for (i=1; i<=10; i++)
sum=sum+i;
printf("sum of natural numbers from 1 to
10 is %d\n",sum);
getch( );
}
```

13. Program to accept a number and print mathematical table of the given no.

```c
# include <stdio.h>
# include <conio.h>
main( )
{
int i,t;
clrscr( );
printf("which table u want:");
scanf("%d",&t);
for (i=1; i<=10; i++)
printf("\n%d*%d=%d",t,i,i*t);
getch( );
}
```

14. Program to print 1 to 10 mathematical tables

```c
# include <stdio.h>
# include <conio.h>
main( )
{
int i,j;
clrscr( );
for (i=1; i<=10; i++)
for(j=1;j<=10;j++)
printf("\n%d*%d=%d",i,j,i*j);
getch( );
}
```

15. Program to print fibonacci series.

```c
# include <stdio.h>
# include <conio.h>
main( )
{
int a=0,b=1,c=0,i;
clrscr( );
printf("%d",a);
printf("\n%d",b);
for (i=1; i<=10; i++)
{c
=a+b;
printf("\n%d",c);
a=b;
b=c;
}
getch( );
}
```

16. Program to print numeric pyramid

```c
# include <stdio.h>
# include <conio.h>
main()
{
int i,j;
clrscr( );
for(i=1;i<=5;i++)
{
for(j=1;j<=i;j++)
printf("%d",j);
printf("\n");
}
getch();
}
```

17. Program to print numerical pyramid.

```c
# include <stdio.h>
# include <conio.h>
main( )
{
int i,j ,l,k=40;
clrscr( );
for(i=1;i<=9;i+=2)
{
for(l=1;l<=k;l++)
printf(" " );
for(j=1;j<=i;j++);
printf("%d",j);
printf("\n");
k=k-2;
}
getch( );
}
```

18. Program to print numerical diamond.

```c
# include <stdio.h>
# include <conio.h>
main( )
{
int i,j,l,n,s,k=40;
clrscr( );
for(i=1;i<=9;i+=2)
{
for(l=1;l<=k;l++)
printf(" ");
for(j=1;j<=i;j++)
printf("\n");
k=k-2;
}
k=k+4;
for(n=7;n>=1;n-=2)
{
```

```c
for(i=1;i<=k;i++)
printf(" ");
for(s=1;s<n;s++)
printf("%d",s);
printf("\n");
k=k+2;
}
getch( );
}
```

19. Program to print character pyramid.

```c
# include <stdio.h>
# include <conio.h>
main( )
{
char i,j;
clrscr();
for(i=65;i<=70;i++)
{
for(j=65;j<=i;j++)
printf("%c",j);
printf("\n");
}
getch( );
}
```

20.   Program to print character diamond.

```c
# include <stdio.h>
# include <conio.h>
main( )
{
char i,j,n,r;
int s,sp=40;
clrscr( );
for(i=65;i<=75;i+=2)
{
for(s=1;s<=sp;s++)
printf(" ");
for(j=65;j<i;j++)
printf("%c",j);
printf("\n");
sp=sp-2;
}
sp=sp+4;
```

```c
for(n=73;n>=65;n-=2)
{
for(s=1;s<=sp;s++)
printf(" ");
for(r=65;r<=n;r++)
printf("%c",r);
sp=sp+2;
}
getch( );
}
```

21. Program to find biggest of two no by using ternary numbers

```c
# include <stdio.h>
# include <conio.h>
main( )
{
int a,b,big;
clrscr( );
printf("enter value a");
scanf("%d",&a);
printf("enter the value of b");
scanf("%d",&b);
big=(a>b)?a:b;
printf("biggest of the given numbers IS
%d",big);
getch();
}
```

22. Program to find biggest of four no by using ternary numbers

```c
# include <stdio.h>
# include <conio.h>
main( )
{
int a,b,c,d,big;
clrscr( );
printf("enter value a");
scanf("%d",&a);
printf("enter the value of b");
scanf("%d",&b);
printf("enter the value of c");
scanf("%d",&c);
printf("enter the value of d");
scanf("%d",&d);
big=(a>b)?(a>c)?(a>d)?a:d:(c>d)?c:d:(b>c
)?(b>d)?b:d:(c>d)?c:d;
printf("biggest of the given 4 numbers IS
```

```c
%d",big);
getch();

}
```

23. Program to print smallest of four no by using ternary operators

```c
# include <stdio.h>
# include <conio.h>
main( )
{
int a,b,c,d,small;
clrscr( );
printf("enter value a");
scanf("%d",&a);
printf("enter the value of b");
scanf("%d",&b);
printf("enter the value of c");
scanf("%d",&c);
printf("enter the value of d");
scanf("%d",&d);
small=(a<b)?(a<c)?(a<d)?a:d:(c<d)?c:d:(b
<c)?(b<d)?b:d:(c<d)?c:d;
printf("biggest of the given 4 numbers IS
```

```c
%d",small);
getch();
}
```

24. Program to accept a year and check the given year is leap or not by using ternary

```c
# include <stdio.h>
# include <conio.h>
main( )
{
int y,leap;
clrscr( );
printf("enter any yr");
scanf("%d",&y);
leap=(y%400= =0)?:(y%100!=0)?(y%4= =0)?1:0:0;
if(leap= =1)
printf(" the given year is leap year");
else
printf("given year is not leap year);
getch( );
}
```

25. Program to accept a character in the uppercase and print in lower case.

```
# include <stdio.h>
# include <conio.h>
main( )
{
char ch,c1;
clrscr( );
printf("enter a cha in uppercase");
ch=getchar();
c1=ch+32;
printf("the given char in lowercasecase
is");
putchar(c1);
getch();
}
```

26. Program to accept a character in any case and print in another case.

```c
# include <stdio.h>
# include <conio.h>
main( )
{
char ch,c1;
clrscr( );
printf("enter a char in anycase");
ch=getchar();
if(ch>=65 && ch<=90)
c1=ch+32;
else
if(ch>=97 && ch<=122)
c1=ch-32;
printf("the given char in anothercase IS");
putchar(c1);
getch();
}
```

27. Program to natural number from 1 to 10 by using while loop.

```c
# include <stdio.h>
# include <conio.h>
main( )
{
int a=0;
clrscr();
while( a<10)
{
a=a+1;
printf("%d\n",a);
}
getch();
}
```

28. Program to accept a string and print it by using the while loop.

```c
# include <stdio.h>
# include <conio.h>
main( )
{
char ch;
clrscr();
printf("enter a string");
while(( ch=getchar( ))!='\n')
putchar(ch);
getch();
}
```

29. Program to accept a string in upper case and print it by lower case.

```c
# include <stdio.h>
# include <conio.h>
main( )
{
char ch,c;
clrscr();
printf("enter a string in upper case:");
while(( ch=getchar( ))!='\n')
{
c=ch+32;
putchar(c);
}
printf(" is in lower case");
getch( );
}
```

30. Program to accept a string in any case and print it by another case .

```c
# include <stdio.h>
# include <conio.h>
main( )
{
char ch;
clrscr( );
printf("enter a string :");
while(( ch=getchar( ))!='\n')
{
if(ch>='A' && ch<='Z')
putchar(ch+32);
else
if(ch>='a' && ch<='z')
putchar(ch-32);
else
putchar(ch);
}
```

```c
printf(" is the string");
getch( );
}
```

31. Program to accept a string print each word in new line.

```c
# include <stdio.h>
# include <conio.h>
main( )
{
char ch;
clrscr( );
printf("enter a string :");
while(( ch=getchar( ))!='\n')
{
putchar(ch);
if(ch= =' ')
printf("\n");
}
getch( );
}
```

32. Program to accept a string and count no of capital letters, no. of small letters and no. of special characters

```c
# include <stdio.h>
# include <conio.h>
main( )
{
char ch;
int c=0,s=0,s1=0;
clrscr( );
printf("enter a string :");
while(( ch=getchar( ))!='\n')
{
if(ch>='A'&& ch>='Z')
c=c+1;
else
if(ch>='a'&& ch>='z')
s=s+1;
```

```
else
s1=s1+1;
}
printf(" no of capital letters are %d",c);
printf(" no of small letters are %d",s);
printf(" no of special characters are
%d",s1);
getch( );
}
```

33. Program to accept any single digit number and print it in words.

```c
# include <stdio.h>
# include <conio.h>
main( )
{
int n;
clrscr( );
printf("enter a number :");
scanf("%d ",&n);
switch(n)
{
case 0: printf("ZERO");
break;
case 1: printf("ONE");
break;
case 2: printf("TWO");
break;
case 3: printf("THREE");
```

```c
break;
case 4: printf("FOUR");
break;
case 5: printf("FIVE");
break;
case 6: printf("SIX");
break;
case 7: printf("SEVEN");
break;
case 8: printf("EIGHT");
break;
case 9: printf("NINE");
break;
default:
printf("please enter the number between 0
and 9");
}
getch( );
}
```

34. Program to print prime numbers between 1 to 100

```c
# include <stdio.h>
# include <conio.h>
main( )
{
int n, i, check;
clrscr();
for(i=1;i<=100;i++)
{
check=1;
for(n=2;n<=i/2;n++)
if(i%n= =0)
{
check=0;
break;
}
if(check= =1)
printf("\n %d is a prime",i);
```

```c
else

printf("\n %d is not a prime",i);

}

getch( );

}
```

35. Program to accept two numbers and print sum of two numbers by using functions

```c
# include <stdio.h>
# include <conio.h>
main( )
{
int a,b,c;
clrscr();
printf("enter the value for a:")
scanf("%d",&a);
printf("enter the value for b:")
scanf("%d",&b);
c=add(a,b);
printf("sum of two numbers is %d",c);
getch( );
}
int add(int x, int y)
{
```

```
int z;

z=x+y;

return z;

}
```

36. Program to accept a number and find factorial of given number

```c
# include <stdio.h>
# include <conio.h>
main( )
{
int n,f;
clrscr( );
printf("enter a number:")
scanf("%d",&n);
f= fact(n);
printf("factorial value is %d",f);
getch();
}
int fact(int n)
{
int i, fa=1;
for(i=n;i>=1;i--)
fa=fa*i;
```

```
    return fa;
}
```

37. Program to accept a number and check the given number Armstrong or not

```c
# include <stdio.h>
# include <conio.h>
main( )
{
int n,arm;
clrscr();
printf("enter any 3 digit number:")
scanf("%d",&n);
arm= armstrong(n);
if(arm= =n)
printf("%d is Armstrong number",n);
else
printf("%d not a Armstrong number",n);
getch( );
}
int Armstrong (int n)
```

```
{
int a,b,c,d;
a=n/100;
b=((n/10)%10);
c=n%10;
d=a*a*a+b*b*b+c*c*c;
return d;
}
```

38. Program to accept a number and print the sum of given and Reverse number

```c
# include <stdio.h>
# include <conio.h>
main( )
{
int a,b,n;
clrscr( );
printf("enter a number:")
scanf("%d",&n);
a=rev(n);
printf("REVERSE OF A GIVEN
NUMBER IS %d",a);
b=add(n,a);
printf("\n sum of a given and reverse
number is %d",b);
getch( );
}
```

```c
int rev( int n)
{
int r,rev=0,s;
while(n>0)
{r
=n%10;
rev=rev*10+r;
n=n/10;
}r
eturn rev;
}
int add(int n, int a)
{
return n+a;
}
```

39. Program to accept 10 numbers and print first five numbers in original order and print last five numbers in reverse order.

```c
# include <stdio.h>
# include <conio.h>
main( )
{
int i,a[10];
for(i=0;i<10;i++)
{
printf("enter value for a[%d]",i);
scanf("%d",&a[i]);
}
for(i=0;i<=4;i++)
printf("\nA[%d]=%d",i,a[i]);
for(i=9;i>=5;i--)
printf("\nA[%d]=%d",i,a[i]);
getch( );
```

}

40. Program to accept a string and print the reverse of the given string by using for loop.

```c
# include <stdio.h>
# include <conio.h>
main( )
{
int i,j;
char name[80];
clrscr( );
printf(" enter a string");
gets(name);
for(i=0;i<80 && ((name [i]=
getchar())!='\n');i++);
if(name[i]= ='\n')
name[i]='\0';
for(j=i;j>=0;j--)
putchar(name[j]);
printf("is the reverse of given string");
```

```
getch( );
}
```

41. Program to accept a string and check the given string is palindrome or not .

```c
# include <stdio.h>
# include <conio.h>
main( )
{
int i,lim,c,check=1;
char word[80];
clrscr( );
printf(" enter a string");
for(i=0;i<80 && ((word [i]=
getchar()) != '\n');i++);
lim=i-1;
c=lim/2;
for(i=0;i<=0;i++,lim--)
if(word[i]!= word[lim])
{
check=0;
```

```c
        break;

    }

    if(check= =1)

        printf("the given string is palindrome ");

    else

        printf(" not palindrome");

    getch( );

}
```

42. Program to accept values into 3 dimensional array and print.

```c
# include <stdio.h>
# include <conio.h>
main( )
{
int a[3][3],i,j;
clrscr( );
for(i=0;i<=2;i++)
for(j=0;j<=2;j++)
{
printf(" enter the value for a[%d][%d]
:",i,j);
scanf("%d",&a[i][j]);
}
for(i=0;i<=2;i++)
{
for(j=0;j<=2;j++)
printf(" %d:",a[i][j]);
```

```c
printf('\n");
}
getch( );
}
```

43. Program to print upper triangle.

```c
# include <stdio.h>
# include <conio.h>
main( )
{
int a[4][4],i,j,c;
clrscr( );
printf(" enter which no u want");
scanf("%d",&c);
for(i=0;i<4;i++)
for(j=0;j<4;j++)
if(i<j)
a[i][j]=c;
else
a[i][j]=0;
for(i=0;i<4;i++)
for(j=0;j<4;j++)
{
printf(" %d:",a[i][j]);
printf('\n");
```

```
   }
getch( );
   }
```

44. Program to accept two 3 dimensional array and store addition of those into arrays into the third array.

```c
# include <stdio.h>
# include <conio.h>
main( )
{
int a[3][3],b[3][3],c[3][3],i,j;
clrscr( );
for(i=0;i<3;i++)
for(j=0;j<3;j++)
{
printf("enter the two values for
a[%d][%d] & b[%d][%d]", i,j,i,j);
scanf("%d%d",&a[i][j],&b[i][j]);
}
for(i=0;i<3;i++)
```

```c
{
for(j=0;j<3;j++)
{
c[i][j]=a[i][j]+b[i][j];
printf("%d",c[i][j]);
}
printf("\n");
}
getch( );
}
```

45. Program to accept a string and find the length of the given string by using functions

```c
# include <stdio.h>
# include <conio.h>
int getline(char str[]);
main( )
{
char str[80];
int length;
clrscr( );
printf(" enter a string");
length=getline(str);
printf("length of the given string is
%d",length);
getch ( );
}
int getline(char str[])
{
```

```
int i;
for(i=0;i<80&&((str[i]=getchar( ))!='\n');
i++);
if(str[i]= ='\n')
str[i]='\0';
return i;
}
```

46. Program to count the number of words, characters, alphabets, vowels, consonants and digit in a line of text.

```
#include<stdio.h>
#include<conio.h>
main( )
{
int noa=0,nob=0,noc=0,nov=0,now=0,noch=0,l,I;
char ch,s[100];
clrscr( );
printf("enter 2 lines of text");
gets(s);
l=strlen(s);
for(i=0;i<1;i++)
{
switch(s[i])
{c
ase 'a':
case 'e':
```

```c
        case 'i':
        case 'o':
        case 'u':
        case 'A':
        case 'E':
        case 'I':
        case 'O':
        case 'U':
        nov++;
        break;
        }
        if(isalpha(s[i]))
        noa++;
        if(isdigit(s[i]))
        nod++;
        if(noa[i]==' ') && (noa[i+1]!=' ')
        now++;
        }
        noch=l-nob;
        noc=noa-nov;
        printf(total no of words %d",now);
```

```c
printf(total no of characters(without blanks)%d",noch);
printf(total no of characters(including blanks)%d",l);
printf(total no of alphabets %d",noa);
printf(total no of vowels %d",nov);
printf(total no of characters %d",noc);
printf(total no of digits %d",nod);
getch( );
}
```

47. Program to accept two string and compare the strings are equal or not

```c
# include <stdio.h>
# include <conio.h>
int getline (char line[ ], int lim );
int strc(char str1[ ], char str2[] );
main( )
{
char str1[80],str2[80];
int comp;
clrscr( );
printf("enter first string:");
getline(str1,80);
printf("enter second string:");
getline(str2,80);
comp=strc(str1,str2);
if(comp>0)
printf("first string is bigger");
```

```c
else
if(comp==0)
printf("both the strings are equal");
getch( );
}
int getline(char str[], int lin)
{
int i;
for(i=0;i<lin&&((str[i]=getchar())!='\n');i++);
if(str[i]='\0')
return i;
}
int strc(char str1[],char str2[])
{
int i;
for(i=0;str1[i];i++)
if(str1[i]!=str2[i])
return str1[i]-str2[i];
return str1[i]-str2[i];
}
```

48. Program to sort the entered numbers using bubble sort.

```c
# include <stdio.h>
# include <conio.h>
main( )
{
int a[100],i,j,n,t;
clrscr( );
printf("enter the array size");
scanf("%d",&n);
for(i=1;i<n;i++)
scanf("%d",&a[i]);
for(i=1;i<=n;i++)
for(j=i+1;j<n;j++)
if(a[i]>a[j])
{
t=a[i]
a[i]=a[j];
a[j]=t;
```

```c
}
printf("the sorted elements are ");
for(i=1;i<=n;i++)
print("%d",a[i]);
getch( );
}
```

49. Program to read date,month, year and print the next day's date,month,year.

```c
# include <stdio.h>
# include <conio.h>
main( )
{
int
month[12]={31,28,31,30,31,30,31,31,30,31,30,31};
int d,m,y,nd,nm,ny,ndays;
clrscr( );
printf("enter the date,month,year");
scanf("%d%d%d",&d,&m,&y);
ndays=month[m-1];
if(m==2)
{
if(y%100==0)
{
```

```c
if(y%400==0)
ndays=29;
}
else
if(y%4==0)
ndays=29;
}
nd=nd+1;
nm=m;
ny=y;
if(nd>ndays)
{
nd=1;
nm++;
}
if(nm>12)
{
nm=1;
ny++;
}
printf("Given date is
```

```
%d:%d:%d\n",d,m,y);
printf("next days date is
%d:%d:%d",nd,nm,ny);
getch( );
}
```

50. Program to interchange two values using pointers.

```c
# include <stdio.h>
# include <conio.h>
void interchange(int *x,int *y);
main( )
{
int a,b;
clrscr( );
printf("enter values of a and b");
scanf("%d%d",&a,&b);
interchange(&a,&b);
}
void interchange(x,y)
int *x,*y;
{
int t;
t=*x;
*x=*y;
```

```c
*y=t;
printf("%d=x, %d=y",*x,*y);
getch( );
}
```

51. Program to print "PASCAL TRIANGLE".

```c
#include<stdio.h>
#include<conio.h>
main()
{
int n,p=1,q,num,sp;
clrscr( );
printf("enter the number of rows");
scanf("%d",&n);
for(p=0;p<=n;p++)
{
for(sp=1;sp<=40-(3*p);sp++)
printf(" ");
for(q=0;q<n;q++)
{
if((q==q)||(q==0))
num=1;
else
```

```c
num=num*((q-q)+1)/q;
printf("%2d",num);
printf("\n");
}}
getch( );
}
```

52. Program to check whether a given number is perfect or not.

```c
# include <stdio.h>
# include <conio.h>
main( )
{
int i,n,s=0;
clrscr();
printf("enter the number");
scanf("%d",&n);
for(i=1;i<n/2;i++)
if(n%i==0)
s+=i;
if(s= =n)
printf("the number is perfect no");
else
printf("the number is not perfect ");
getch( );
}
```

53. Program to check whether a given number is prime number.

```c
# include <stdio.h>
# include <conio.h>
main( )
{
int i,n,c=0;
clrscr( );
printf("enter a number");
scanf("%d",&n);
for(i=0;i<=n;i++)
if(n%i==0)
c++;
if(c==2)
printf("given number is a prime number");
else
printf("given number is not prime number");
getch( );
```

}

54. Program to read 'n' number and print them in matrix terms in all orders.

```c
# include <stdio.h>
# include <conio.h>
main( )
{
int i,n,c,p,q,r,k,a[20];
clrscr();
printf("enter the array size");
scanf("%d",&n);
printf("enter the elements");
for(i=1;i<=n;i++)
scanf("%d",&a[i]);
i=1;
while(i<=n)
{
if(n%i==0)
{r
```

```c
=i;
c=n/i;
k=1;
for(p=1;p<=r;p++)
{
for(q=1;q<=c;q++)
printf("%d",a[k++])
printf("\n");
}
i++;
getch( );
}
```

55. Program to search an element using binary search

```c
# include <stdio.h>
# include <conio.h>
main( )
{
int a[100],i,n,x, mid, top, bot,c;
clrscr();
printf("enter the array size;");
scanf("%d",&n);
printf("enter the array elements");
for(i=1;i<=n;i++)
scanf("%d",&a[i]);
top=1;
bot=n;
c=0;
printf("enter the element to searched");
scanf("%d",&x);
while((top <=bot)&&(c==0))
```

```c
{
mid=(top+bot)/2;
if(a[mid]<x)
top=mid+1;
else
if(a[mid]>x)
bot=mid-1;
else
c=1;
}
if(c==1)
printf("elements is at position;%d",mid);
else
printf("elements is not in list");
getch( );
}
```

56. Program to accept two numbers and print the sum of given two numbers by using pointers

```c
# include <stdio.h>
# include <conio.h>
main( )
{
int a, b,c;
clrscr( );
a=10;
b=20;
c=*(&a)+*(&b);
printf("%d",c);
getch( );
}
```

57. Programs to multiply two Matrices

```c
# include <stdio.h>
# include <conio.h>
main( )
{
int
a[10][10],b[10][10],c[10],[10],i,j,m,n,p,q,
k;
clrscr( );
printf("enter the size of first matrices");
scanf("%d%d',&m,&n);
printf("enter the size of second matrix");
scanf("%d%d',&p,&q);
if(n==p)
{
printf("enter first matrices elements");
for(i=1;i<m;i++)
for(j=1;j<n;j++)
```

```c
scanf("%d",&a[i][j]);
printf("enter second matrix elements");
for(i=1;i<p;i++)
for(j=1;j<q;j++)
scanf("%d",&b[i][j]);
for(i=1;i<m;i++)
for(j=1;j<n;j++)
{
c[i][j]=0;
for(k=1;k<n;k++)
c[i][j]=c[i][j]+a[i][k]*b[k][j];
}
printf("the multiplication matrix is");
for(i=1;i<m;i++)
{
for(j=1;j<n;j++)
print("%2d",c[i][j]);
printf("\n");
}
}
else
```

```c
printf("multiplication is not possible");
getch( );
}
```

58. Program to print prime number between 1-100

```c
# include <stdio.h>
# include <conio.h>
main( )
{
int i,n,c;
clrscr( );
for(n=1;n<=100;n++)
{c
=0;
for(i=1;i<=n;i++)
if(n%i==0)
c++;
if(c==2)
printf("\n%d",n);
}
getch( );
}
```

59. Program to accept a string and find the length of the string

```c
# include <stdio.h>
# include <conio.h>
main( )
{
char name[80];
int i;
clrscr( );
printf("enter a string ;");
for(i=0;i<80&&((name[i]=getchar( ))!
='\n');i++);
printf("%d is the size of string",i);
getch( );
}
```

60. Program to fibanocci of matrix

```c
# include <stdio.h>
# include <conio.h>
# include <math.h>
main( )
{
int a[10][10],i,j,m,n sum=0;
float norm;
clrscr( );
printf('enter the matrix size");
scanf("%d%d",&m,&n);
printf("enter the element of matrix");
for(i=1;i<=m;i++)
for(j=1;j<=n;j++)
{
scanf("%d",&a[i][j]);
sum=sum+(a[i][j]*a[i][j])
}
norm=sqrt(sum);
printf("norm=%f",norm);
```

```
getch( );

}
```

61. Program a structure which reads 'n' students information (name,3 subjects marks) and calculate total marks, result print them in a particular format.

```c
# include <stdio.h>
# include <conio.h>
main( )
{
struct student
{
char name[20];
int m1,m2,m3, tot;
char result[10];
}stud[10];
int i,n;
clrscr( );
printf("enter no of students \n");
scanf("%d",&n);
```

```c
for(i=0;i<n;i++)
{
printf("enter %d student deatails \n",i);
printf("enter name\n");
scanf("%s", stud[i].name);
printf("enter marks of 3 subjects \n");
scanf("%d%d%d",
&stud[i].m1,&stud[i].m2,&stud[i].m3);
stud[i].tot=stud[i].m1+stud[i].m2+stud[i].
m3;
if((stud[i].m1>35)&&(stud[i].m2>35)&&(
stud[i].m3>35))
strcpy(stud[i].result,"pass");
else
strtcpy(stud[i].result,"fail");
}
clrscr( );
printf("name total result \n");
for(i=0;i<n;i++)
{
printf("%s %d %s \n",
```

```
stud[i].name,stud[i].tot,stud[i].result);

}

getch( );

}
```

62. Program to find whether a square matrix is a) symmetric b) skew symmetric c) none of two.

```c
# include <stdio.h>
# include <conio.h>
main( )
{
int a[10][10],i,j,m,n,c=0,c1=0;
clrscr( );
printf("enter the array size");
scanf("%d",&n);
printf("enter the elements");
for(i=1;i<=m;i++)
for(j=1;j<=n;j++)
scanf("%d",&a[i][j]);
for(i=1;i<=m;i++)
for(j=1;j<=n;j++)
{
if(a[i][j]==a[j][i])
c=1;
```

```c
else
if(a[i][j]==a[j][i])
c1=1;
}
printf("the given matrix is \n");
for(i=1;i<=m;i++)
{
for(j=1;j<=n;j++)
printf("%4d",a[i][j]);
printf("\n");
}
if(c==0)
printf("the given matrix is symmetric");
else
if(c1==0)
printf("the matrix is skew symmetric");
else
printf("none of two");
}
getch( );
}
```

63. Program to find area of a triangle when their sides are given.

```c
# include <stdio.h>
# include <conio.h>
main( )
{
int a,b,c;
float s, area;
clrscr( );
printf("enter there sides of the triangle");
scanf("%d%d%d",&a,&b,&c);
if((a+b)<c||(b+c)<a||(a+c)<b)
printf("finding area is not possible");
else
s=(a+b+c)/2;
area=sqrt(s*(s-a)*(s-b)*(s-c));
printf("area=%.2f",area);
getch( );
}
```

64. Program to print Armstrong number between 1-500.

```c
#include<stdio.h>
#include <conio.h>
main( )
{
int i,n,s,r;
clrscr( );
for(i=1;i<=500;i++)
{
n=i;
s=0;
while(n>0)
{r
=n%10;
s=s+(r*r*r);
n=n/10;
}
if(i==s)
```

```
printf("\n%d",s);

}

getch();

}
```

65. Program to check whether a given number is Armstrong or not.

```c
# include <stdio.h>
# include <conio.h>
main( )
{
int i,n,s,r,k;
clrscr( );
printf("enter a number");
scanf("%d",&n);
k=n;
s=0;
while(n>0)
{r
=n%10;
s=s+(r*r*r);
n=n/10;
}
if(k==s)
```

```c
printf("given number is Armstrong
%d",k);
else
printf("given number is not Armstrong
%d",k);
}
getch();
}
```

66. Program to print the floyd's triangle.

```c
# include <stdio.h>
# include <conio.h>
main( )
{
int i,n,s,r k=1;
clrscr( );
printf("enter a number of rows");
scanf("%d",&n);
for(i=1;i<=n;i++)
{
for(s=1;s<=40-i;s++)
printf(" ");
for(j=1;j<=i;j++)
printf("%3d",k++);
printf("\n");
}
getch( );
}
```

67. Program to read data in 3 structures and print

```c
# include<stdio.h>
# include<conio.h>
main( )
{
struct book
{
char code;
int piece;
float price;
};
struct book b1,b2,b3;
main( )
{
clrscr( );
printf("enter code,piece,price");
scanf("%c%d%f",&b1.code,&b1.piece,&b1.price);
printf("enter code,piece,price");
```

```c
scanf("%c%d%f",&b2.code,&b2.piece,&b2.price);
printf("enter code,piece,price");
scanf("%c%d%f",&b3.code,&b3.piece,&b3.price);
printf("the details are");
printf("\n %c%d%f",b1.code,b1.piece,b1.price);
printf("\n %c%d%f",b2.code,b2.piece,b2.price);
printf("\n %c%d%f",b3.code,b3.piece,b3.price);
getch( );
}
```

68. Program to print a diagonal matrix.

```c
#include<conio.h>
#include<stdio.h>
main()
{
int a[4][4],i,j;
clrscr( );
for(i=0;i<4;i++)
for(j=0;j<4;j++)
if(i==j)
c[i][j]=7;
else
a[i][j]=0;
for(i=0;i<4;i++)
{
for(j=0;j<4;j++)
printf("%d",a[i][j]);
printf("\n");
```

```
   }
getch();
   }
```

69. Program to copy contents of one file into another.

```c
#include<stdio.h>
#include<conio.h>
main( )
{
FILE *fp1,*fp2;
char ch;
fp1=fopen("text1","w");
printf('enter the text");
while((ch=getchar( ))!=EOF)
putc(ch,fp1);
fclose(fp1);
fp1=fopen("text1","r");
fp2=fopen("text2","w");
while((ch=getc(fp1))!=EOF)
putc(ch,fp2);
fclose(fp2);
getch( );
}
```

70. Program to create a file of number and copy odd number into second file and even number into third file.

```c
#include<stdio.h>
#include<conio.h>
main( )
{
FILE *fp1,*fp2,*fp3;
int i;
fp1=fopen("DATA1","w");
printf("enter the number");
scanf("%d",&i);
while(i!=eof( ))
{
putw(i,fp1);
}f
colse(fp1);
fp1=fopen("DATA1","r");
```

```c
fp2=fopen("DATA2","w");
fp3=fopen("DATA3","w");
while((i=getw(fp1))!=EOF())
if(i%2= =0)
putw(i,fp3);
else
putw(i,fp2);
fcolse(fp1);
fcolse(fp2);
fcolse(fp3);
getch( );
}
```

71. Program a structure which stores information about hotels which stores information about name, grade, room change, no of rooms.

a) Print the hotels of given grade in order of roomchange.

b) Print the hotels with roomchange less than a given change.

```c
#include<stdio.h>
#include<conio.h>
main( )
{
struct hotel
{
char name[20];
char city[10];
char grade;
```

```c
int rc,nr;
};
struct hotel ht[20],t;
int i,n,j,c;
char gr;
clrscr( );
printf("enter no. of hotels\n");
scanf("%d",&n);
for(i=0;i<n;i++)
{
printf("enter name of hotel \n");
scanf("%s",&ht[i].name);
printf("enter name of city \n");
scanf("%s",&ht[i].city);
printf("enter the grade \n");
scanf("%s".ht[i].grade);
ht[i].grade=getche( );
printf("enter room charge \n");
scanf("%d",&ht[i].rc);
printf("enter no of rooms \n");
scanf("%d",&ht[i].nr);
```

```c
}
for(i=0;i<n;i++)
for(j=0;j<n-i;j++)
{
t=ht[j];
ht[j]=ht[j+i];
ht[j+1]=t;
}
printf("enter a grade to print the hotels
\n");
gr=getche();
clrscr();
printf("hotel name city grade roomcharge
no of room");
for(i=0;i<n;i++)
if(gr==ht[i].grade)
printf("%s %s %c %d
%d",ht[i].name,ht[i].city,ht[i].grade,ht[i].r
c,ht[i].nr);
getch();
printf("enter a room charge to print hotels
```

```c
less than given charge \n");
scanf("%d",&c);
printf("hotel name city grade roomcharge
no of rooms");
for(i=0;i<n;i++)
if(c<=ht[i].rc)
printf("%s %s %c %d
%d",ht[i].name,ht[i].city,h[i].grade,ht[i].rc
,ht[i].nr);
}
```

72. Program which does the below process after reading on odd no of integer.

a)Print them in given order.

b)Replace second elements by product of first and last element

c)Replace middle value by average of all elements.

d)Replace all –ve no's by zero's.

```c
#include<stdio.h>
#include<conio.h>
main( )
{
int a[10],i,n,sum=0;
clrscr( );
```

```c
printf("enter the array sixe ");
scanf("%d",&n);
printf("enter the elements");
for(i=0;i<n;i++)
{
scanf("%d",&a[i]);
sum=sum+a[i];
}
printf("The given arrays is: ");
for(i=0;i<n;i++)
printf("%d",a[i]);
a[2]=a[1]*a[n-1];
printf("\n the given areay after replacing
2nd element is");
for(i=0;i<n;i++)
printf("%d",a[i]);
a[(1+n/2)]=sum/n;
printf("\n the given array after replacing
middle element by average of all");
for(i=0;i<n;i++)
if(a[i]<0)
```

```c
a[i]=0;
printf("\n given array after replacing –ve values by zero");
for(i=0;i<n;i++)
printf("%d",a[i]);
printf("\n");
getch();
}
```

73. Program to sort the entered elements using selection sort technique.

```
#include<stdio.h>

#include<conio.h>

main( )

{

int a[100],i,n,j,t,min,pos;

clrscr();

printf("enter the array size");

scanf("%d",&n);

printf("enter the elements");

for(i=0;i<n;i++)

scanf("%d",&a[i]);

for(i=0;i<n;i++)

{

min=a[i];

pos=i;

for(j=0;j<n-1;j++)
```

```c
if(min>a[j])
{
min=j;
pos=j;
}
t=a[i];
a[i]=a[pos];
a[pos]=t;
}
printf("the sorted elements are");
for(i=0;i<n;i++)
printf("%2d",a[i]);
getch( );
}
```

74. Program to find whether a number is divisible by '11' or not without actual division.

```c
#include<stdio.h>
#include<conio.h>
#include<math.h>
main( )
{
int a,b,n,evensum=0,oddsum=0,div;
clrscr( );
printf("enter a number");
scanf("%d",&n);
a=n;
b=n/10;
while(a>0)
{
oddsum=oddsum+(a%10);
a=a/10;
}
```

```c
while(b>0)
{
evensum=evensum+(b%10);
b=b/10;
}
div=abs(evensum-oddsum);
if(div%11==0)
printf("The number is divisible by 11");
else
printf("The number is not divisible by 11");
getch();
}
```

75. Program to find maximum and minimum of entered 'n' number using arrays.

```c
#include<stdio.h>
#include<conio.h>
main( )
{
int i,n,a[10],min,max;
clrscr( );
printf(" enter how many number");
scanf("%d",&n);
printf("enter the elements");
for(i=0;i<n;i++)
scanf("%d",&a[i]);
min=a[0];
for(i=0;i<n;i++)
if(min>a[i])
min=a[i];
printf("minimum=%d",min);
```

```c
max=0;
for(i=0;i<n;i++)
if(max<a[i]);
max=a[i];
printf("\n maximum=%d",max);
getch( );
}
```

76. Program to print the following series until there sum exceeds 2.6 term value exceeds 1.5

$$x+x2/2!+x3/3!+-----------.$$

```c
#include<stdio.h>
#include<conio.h>
main( )
{
float x,sum=0,prod=1;
int i;
clrscr( );
printf("enter x value");
scanf("%f",&x);
i=1;
while((sum<2.6)&&(prod<=1.5))
{
prod=prod*(x/i);
if(prod<=1.5)
sum=sum+prod;
```

```c
if(sum>2.6)
{
sum=sum-prod;
break;
}
printf("sum=;%f",sum);
i++;
}
getch( );
}
```

77. Program to print a frequency distribution table for a class of 20-students in the following format. The marks range form 1-25. class intertval frequency

```c
#include<stdio.h>
#include<conio.h>
main( )
{
int a[20],i,n1=0,n2=0,n3=0,n4=0,n5=0;
clrscr();
printf("enter the any 20 no of range(1-
25));
for(i=1;i<=20;i++)
scanf("%d",&a[i]);
for(i=1;i<=20;i++)
if((a[i]>=1)&&(a[i]<6))
n1++;
else
```

```c
if((a[i]>5)&&(a[i]<11))
n2++;
else
if((a[i]>10)&&(a[i]<16))
n3++;
else
if((a[i]>15)&&(a[i]<21))
n4++;
else
if((a[i]>20)&&(a[i]<26))
n5++;
printf("class interval frequency");
printf("\n 1-5 %d",n1);
printf("\n 6-10 %d",n2);
printf("\n 11-15 %d",n3);
printf("\n 16-20 %d",n4);
printf("\n 21-25 %d",n5);
getch();
}
```

78. Program to accept values into an array and print array in reverse and original format by using three different functions.

```
#include<stdio.h>
#include<conio.h>
void read_array(int x[]);
void print_array(int y[]);
void rev_array(int z[]);
main()
{
int a[5];
clrscr();
read_array(a);
printf_array(a);
rev_array(a);
getch( );
}
void read_array(int x[])
```

```c
{
int i;
for(i=0;i<=4;i++)
{
printf("enter values for a[%d]:",i);
scanf("%d",&x[i]);
}}
void print_array(int y[])
{
int i;
for(i=0;i<=4;i++)
printf("%d",y[i]);
}
void rev_array(int z[])
{
int i;
for(i=4;i>=0;i--)
printf("\n%d",z[i]);
}
```

79. Program to accept values into single dimensional array and print the array in reverse by using pointers.

```c
#include<stdio.h>
#include<conio.h>
main( )
{
int a[5],*b,i;
clrscr( );
b=&a[0];
for(i=0;i<=4;i++)
{
printf("enter a value for a[%d];".i);
scanf("%d",b);
b++;
}
b=&a[4];
for(i=0;i<=4;i++)
```

```c
{
printf("\n%d",*b);
b-- ;
}
getch( );
}
```

80. Program to read a string and print the number of characters in each word of the string.

```c
#include<stdio.h>
#include<conio.h>
#include<string.h>
main( )
{
char s[100];
int i,l,nc=0;
clrscr( );
printf("enter the sting");
gets(s);
l=strlen(s);
for(i=0;i<l;i++)
{
if(s[i]!=' ')
{
nc=0;
```

```c
while(s[i]!=' ')
{
nc++;
printf("%c",s[i]);
i++;
if(s[i]='\0')
break;
}
printf("\t\t %d",nc);
printf("\n");
}} getch();
}
```

81. Program to accept two strings and compare those two strings

```c
#include<stdio.h>
#include<conio.h>
int strcomp (char *pt1, char *pt2);
void read-string(char*pt);
main( )
{
char line [80],line2[80];
clrscr( );
printf("enter first string;");
read-string (line1);
printf("enter second string");
read-string(line2);
if(strcomp (line1,line2)>0)
printf("second string biggest");
else
if(strcomp (line1,line2)>0)
printf(" first string biggest;");
```

```c
else
printf("both the strins are equal");
getch( );
}
void read-string(char*pt)
{
for(;(*pt=getchar( ))!='\n';pt++);
*pt='\0';
}
int strcomp (char *pt1, char *pt2)
{
for(;*pt1!='\0';pt1++;pt2++)
if(*pt1!=*pt2)
break;
return *pt1-*pt2;
}
```

82. Program to accept a string using pointers and functions.

```c
#include<stdio.h>
#include<conio.h>
main( )
{
int ch[20];
clrscr ( );
printf("enter a string");
read_array(ch);
printf("%s",ch);
getch( );
}
void read_string (char*pt)
{
for(;(*pt=getchar( ))!='/n';pt++);
*pt='\0';
}
```

83. Program to read a string and print the first two characters of each word in the string.

```c
#include<stdio.h>
#include<conio.h>
main( )
{
char s[100];
int i,l;
clrscr( );
printf("enter a string");
gets(s);l=strlen(s);
for(i=0;i<l;i++)
{
if(s[i]!=' ' && s[i]=' ')
{
printf("%c %c",s[i],s[i+1])
i=i+2;
while(s[i]!=' ')
```

```
i++;
}}
getch( );
}
```

84. Program to accept two numbers and print the sum of given two numbers by using pointers

```c
#include<stdio.h>
#include<conio.h>
main( )
{
int a, b,c;
clrscr( );
a=10;
b=20;
c=*(&a)+*(&b);
printf("%d",c);
getch( );
}
```

85. Program to accept a string and print reverse of the given string by using functions.

```c
#include<stdio.h>
#include<stdio.h>
int getline (char str[]);
void printline (char str[],int i);
main( )
{
char str[80];
int 1;
clrscr( );
1=getline(str );
printline(str,1);
printline(str,1);
getch ( );
}
int getline(char str[])
{
```

```
int 1;
printf("enter a string;");
for(i=0;i<80&&((str[i]=getchar())!='\n');i++);
if(str[i]='\0';
return i;
}
void printline(char str[],int 1)
{
int j;
for(j=1;j<=0;j--)
printf("%c",str[j]);
printf('is the revefrse string");
}
```

86. Program to accept two 3 dimensional array and store subtraction of those two arrays into third array.

```c
#include<stdio.h>
#include<conio.h>
main( )
{
int a[3][3],b[3][3],c[3][3],i,j;
clrscr( );
for(i=0;i<3;i++)
for(j=0;j<3;j++)
{
printf("enter two values for a[%d][%d] &
b[%d][%d]:",i,j,i,j);
scanf("%d%d",&a[i][j],&b[i][j]);
}
for(i=0;i<3;i++)
{
```

```c
for(j=0;j<3;j++)
{
c[i][j]=a[i][j]-b[i][j];
printf("%d",,c[i][j]);
}
printf("\n");
}
getch( );
```

87. Program to accept a single dimensional array and print them by using pointers

```c
#include<stdio.h>
#include<conio.h>
main( )
{
int a[5],*b,i;
clrscr( );
b=&a[0];
for(i=0;i<=4;i++)
{
printf("enter the a value for a[%d]",i)
scanf("%d",b);
b++;
}
b=&a[0];
for(i=0;i<=4;i++)
{
```

```c
printf("\n%d",*b);

b++;

}

getch( );

}
```

88. Program to accept two strings and biggest among them

```c
#include<stdio.h>
#include<conio.h>
int getline(char line[],int lim);
main( )
{
char str1[80],str2[80];
int len1,len2;
clrscr( );
printf("enter first string");
len1=getline(str1,80);
printf("enter second string");
len2=getline(str1,80);
if(len1 >len2)
printf("first string bigger than second string");
else
if(len1<len2)
printf("second string bigger than first string");
```

```c
else
printf("both strings are equal");
getch( );
}
int getline(char line[],int lim)
{
int i;
for(Ii0;i<lim && ((line[i]=getchar( ))!='\n');i++)
if(line[i]=='\n')
line[i]='\0';
return i;
}
```

89. Program to print 4 dimentional matrix with constant number.

```c
#include<stdio.h>
#include<conio.h>
main( )
{
int a[4][4],i,j,c;
clrscr( );
printf("enter constant number");
scanf("%d",&c);
for(i=0;i<4;i++)
{
for(j=0;j<4;j++)
a[i][j]=c;
for(i=0;i<4;i++)
{
for(j=0;j<4;j++)
printf("%d",a[i][j]);
printf("\n");
```

```
}
getch( );
}
```

90. Program to accept a string and print each word in reverse

```c
#include<conio.h>
#include<stdio.h>
main( )
{
char name[80];
int i,j,start=0,end,len;
clrscr( );
printf("enter a string");
scanf("%s",name);
for(i=0;i<80 &&((name[i]=getchar( ) )!='\n');i++);
len=i;
for(i=0;i<len;i++)
if(name[i]==' '|| name[i]=='\n')
{
end=i;
while((end--)>=start)
{
```

```c
printf("%c",name[end]);
}
start=i+1;
}
getch( );
}
```

91. Program to accept elements into single dimensional array and print the array in ascending order by using three different arrays.

```
#include<conio.h>
#include<stdio.h>
void read_array(int x[]);
void sort_array(int y[]);
void print_array(int z[]);
main()
{
int a[10];
clrscr( );
read_array(a);
sort_array(a);
print_array(a);
getch( );
}
void read_array(int x[])
```

```c
{
int i;
for(i=0;i<10;i++)
{
printf("enter value for a[%d]",i);
scanf("%d",&x[i]);
}}
void sort_array(int y[])
{
int i,j,k;
for(i=0;i<9;i++)
for(j=i+1;j<=9;j++)
if(y[i]>y[j])
{
k=y[i];
y[i]=y[j];
y[j]=k;
}}
void print_array(int z[])
{
int i;
```

```
for(i=0;i<10;i++)
printf("%d\n",z[i]);
}
```

92. Program to accept data and store the given data into file print the data.

```c
#include<conio.h>
#include<stdio.h>
main( )
{
FILE *fp;
char c;
fp=fopen("data.dat","w");
clrscr();
printf("enter text");
while(1)
{c
=getchar( );
if(c==eof( ))
break;
putc(c);
}f
close(fp);
```

```c
fp=fopen("data.dat","r");
while(1)
{c
=getc(fp);
if(c==eof( ))
break;
putchar(c);
}
getch( );
fclose(fp);
}
```

93. Program to accept data in lower case and store the given data into file into upper case and print the data.

```c
#include<conio.h>
#include<stdio.h>
main( )
{
FILE *fp;
Char c;
fp=fopen("data2.dat","w");
clrscr( );
printf("enter text");
while((c=getchar( ))!=eof( ))
{
putc(toupper(c),fp)
}f
close(fp);
fp=fopen("data2.dat","r");
while(1)
```

```c
{c
=getc(fp);
if(c==eof( ))
break;
putchar(c);
}
getch( );
fclose(fp);
}
```

94. Program to copy contents of one file into another.

```c
#include<conio.h>
#include<stdio.h>
main( )
{
FILE * fp1,*fp2;
char ch;
fp1=fopen("text1","w");
printf("enter the text");
while((ch=getchar()!=EOF);
putc(ch,fp1);
fclose(fp1);
fp1=fopen("text1","r");
fp2=fopen("text2","w");
while((ch=getc(fp1))!=EOF)
putc(ch,fp2);
fcolse(fp1);
fcolse(fp2);
```

```
getch( );
}
```

95. Program to create a file of numbers and copy odd number into second file and even number into third file

```
#include<conio.h>
#include<stdio.h>
main( )
{
FILE *fp1,*fp2,*fp3;
int i;
fp1=open("data1","w");
printf("enter the number");
scanf("%d",&i);
while(i!=eof)
{
putw(i,fp1);
scanf("%d",&i);
}f
colse(fp1);
```

```c
fp1=fopen("data1","r");
fp2=fopen("data2","w");
fp3=fopen("data3","w");
while((i=getc(fp1))!=eof)
if(i%2==0)
putc(i,fp3);
else
putw(i,fp2);
fcolse(fp1);
fcolse(fp2);
fcolse(fp3);
getch( );
}
```

96. Program to accept a string in lower case and print first character of each word in upper case.

```c
#include<conio.h>
#include<stdio.h>
main( )
{
char str1[80];
int length,i;
clrscr( );
printf("enter a string; ");
length=getline(str1,80);
for(i=0;i<length;i++)
{
str1[0]-=32;
if(str1[i]==' ')
str1[i+1]-=32;
printf("%c".str1[i]);
}
```

```c
getch();

}

int getline(char line [], int lim)

{

int i;

for(i=0;i<lim && ((line[i]=getchar( ))!
='\n');i++);

if(line[i]= ='\n')

line[i]='\0';

return i;

}
```

97. Program to accept two numbers and interchange two values using functions.

```c
#include<conio.h>
#include<stdio.h>
void swap (int a, int b);
main( )
{
int a,b;
clrscr( );
printf("enter value for a;");
scanf("%d",&a);
printf("enter value for b;");
scanf("%d",&b);
swap(a,b);
getch( );
}
void swap(int a,int b)
{
}
```

```c
int c;
c=a;
a=b;
b=c;
printf("\na=%d",a);
printf("\nb=%d",b);
}
```

98. Program for example of static variable.

```c
#include<conio.h>
#include<stdio.h>
static int i=1;
main( )
{
int j;
clrscr( );
for (j=1;j<=5;j++);
fun( );
getch( );
}
fun( )
{
printf("\n%d",i);
i=i+1;
}
```

99. Program to accept a string and print by trailing spaces.

```c
#include<conio.h>
#include<stdio.h>
main( )
{
char n,n1;
clrscr ( );
printf("enter a string;");
while((n=getchar( )!='\n')
if(n>='a' && n<='z')
putchar(n);
else
if(n>='a' && n<='z')
putchar(n);
getch( );
}
```

100. Program to print anti diagonal.

```c
#include<conio.h>
#include<stdio.h>
main( )
{
int a[4][4],i,j,c;
clrscr( );
printf("enter which number you want;");
scanf("%d",&c);
for(i=0;i<4;i++)
for(j=0;j<4;j++)
if(i+j= =3)
a[i][j]=c;
else
a[i][j]=0
for(i=0;i<4;i++)
{
for(j=0;j<4;j++)
printf("%d",a[i][j]);
printf("\n");
```

```
}

getch( );

}
```

Thank you for reading this ebook.

If you are having any questions, then you can ask me anytime by mail.

My email id: adityashakkarwar@gmail.com

Thank You !!!

www.ingramcontent.com/pod-product-compliance
Lightning Source LLC
Chambersburg PA
CBHW052141070326
40690CB00047B/1348